Joseph Eggleston Segar

Letter of Hon. Joseph Segar, to a Friend in Virginia

In Vindication of His Course in Declining to Follow His State Into Secession

Joseph Eggleston Segar

Letter of Hon. Joseph Segar, to a Friend in Virginia
In Vindication of His Course in Declining to Follow His State Into Secession

ISBN/EAN: 9783337033958

Printed in Europe, USA, Canada, Australia, Japan

Cover: Foto ©ninafisch / pixelio.de

More available books at **www.hansebooks.com**

LETTER

OF

N. JOSEP⬛ ⬛GAR,

TO A FRIEND

IN VINDICA⬛⬛⬛ ⬛⬛ HIS COURSE ⬛⬛ ⬛⬛⬛⬛⬛ FOLLOW HIS
STATE INTO SEC⬛⬛⬛

WASHINGTON, D. C.
WILLIAM H. MOORE, PRINTER.
1862.

LETTER.

Boston, *November* 3, 1861.

My Dear ————

      *   *   *   *   *

You urge me, on account of my distressed wife and children, to return to Virginia, if I can possibly, and with characteristic generosity, you offer to divide with them and me your humble home. God knows that next to peace for our afflicted country, the fondest wish of my heart is to be once more with the loved ones who, as you truly say, once made my home so happy. But we can never meet on the soil of our native land, at least during the continuance of this unhappy war; nor shall we ever, save on some blessed spot where waves that proud emblem of protecting power, the Stars and Stripes.

All considerations of mere personal safety aside, the conditions on which I am advised I may return to Virginia and be safe, are totally inadmissible.

Those conditions are, first, that I go by flag of truce to Norfolk, and there obtain from Gen. Huger a guard of protection; secondly, that under that guard I proceed to Richmond, and there take the oath of allegiance to Virginia before Gov. Letcher; and thirdly, that I also take there before President Davis the oath of allegiance to the Confederate States of America.

I regret that I find it impossible to comply with these hard terms. I can accept no guard from Gen. Huger, nor from any one else who dares, in the land of Washington and Henry, uplift the flag of the Confederate States. When I tread the soil of Virginia, I must tread it free as the air I quaff, with no guard to make me feel the humiliation of a craven slave, with "none to make me afraid."

Still less can I submit to the humiliation of taking the oath of

4

allegiance to the land of my birth. There is no need that I should: I have never been disloyal to my State, no, never. I have but obeyed *her* highest law. She made the Constitution of the United States a part of her own State constitution, and she prescribed that great master-piece of human wisdom to me as a rule of my political conduct, and she prescribed it to me as a *supreme* rule. She gave it to me with two very marked provisions in it: first, that the laws made in pursuance of it should be the supreme law of the land, "any thing in her own State constitution or laws to the contrary notwithstanding;" secondly, that it should not be in any respect changed except by the consent of three-fourths of all the States, in general convention or legislative body assembled.

The first of these provisions is too plain to be misconstrued. It tells me, in terms so plain that school-children may understand, that in a conflict between the Constitution and laws of the United States on the one hand, and those of my State on the other, I must give up the latter and stand by the former. This is just what I am doing. I am obeying my State's commands: I am standing by that higher law which she herself laid down for my guide, and disobedience to which is double disloyalty—disloyalty to her, and disloyalty to the government of the Union, which she, in the plenitude of her power, bade me regard as supreme. Wherein, then, have I been disloyal to my State? She had the undoubted right to issue to me her commands: am I disloyal to her when I execute those commands to the letter?

The second provision quoted is not less explicit. That Constitution which my State prescribed to me as a supreme rule, is not to be altered, as she herself stipulated, except by the assent of three-fourths of all her sister States. Is not this provision as much prescribed to me, and as binding on me, as any other? Did not my State, when she gave me this new rule, order me to guide myself by it; to cling to it; to stand by it and up to it, *until* it should be altered by three-fourths of all the States? Was it not to remain a supreme rule, until thus altered?

This inquiry, then, only arises: *Has* the Constitution been changed by a three-fourths majority? *It has not.* What then? Why this, surely: that *not* having been altered in the only mode in which it can be legally altered, it is binding, *in its original form*, with agreed amendments, upon my State, and upon each and every State, and upon each and every citizen of every State that was living under the Union at the time of its formation, and that has lived under its blessed jurisdiction since. And it will continue to be so binding, until the form of the instrument shall have been changed in the only constitutional mode prescribed.

These two manifest provisions, then, of the Federal Constitution, stamp supremacy upon the Government and laws of the Union, as visibly as the foot-print is impressed on the fresh-fallen snow.

If these positions be well taken, it follows, as the shadow the substance, that if I obey an order of my State to give up and no longer acknowledge the authority of the Federal Government, I allow myself to be made a rebel of, and if I take up arms against it, or give its enemies aid and comfort, a traitor. My State, I devoutly believe, and solemnly protest, has no such prerogative. With all her broad province of authority, she wants the power to make of me a rebel or a traitor, against my consent. At all events, as I, individually, am to be held responsible, and by an all-powerful government, and as, in a case of personal treason, my neck. and not my State's, is to feel the halter's throttle, I have thought myself free to keep on safety's side.

But I am told that my State, as a sovereign State, has the legal right to secede; in other words, to break up the Union at her pleasure ; and that all true and patriotic Virginians are bound to follow her, and will follow her, no matter whither.

This doctrine, so flattering to State pride, I confess I have not been altogether averse to falling into—a thing not very unnatural in a political community in which the Resolutions of '98, with extreme interpretation, alone light the pathway of political aspirants : but it never had from me that assent which is founded in deliberate investigation, and honest conviction. Not until this startling issue of the life or death of the government came upon us, did I discharge the solemn duty to my country of considering. in all its aspects and consequences, this doctrine of separate State secession. I have now examined it fully, and with the sole view of learning where duty pointed me ; and I have reached a conviction unobscured by the shadow of a single doubt, that no obligation to my State binds me to follow in the path which has led her to disunion. She has no constitutional power to release herself or me from the bonds of that paramount allegiance to the Federal Government, with which she bound herself, and me, and all her citizens.

If it be indeed true that the Constitution and laws of the Union are superior to, and overrule the constitution and laws of, the separate States—and if it be further true that it cannot be altered except in a particular mode—which particular mode has not been resorted to—then secession is, irresistibly, an absurdity. Two supreme powers in a governmant are simply impossible, and a power cannot be exercised by a single State which is delegated, without reservation, to three-fourths of a certain number of States—and so this doctrine of secession is whirled down the vortex of a gulf so deep, that no gurgle is heard for its requiem.

And from no such source as the much-boasted one of State sovereignty, can it ever rise into life. Since the Union was formed, there has been in our system no such thing as State sovereignty. It is a myth—a fancy, as ideal as Aladdin's lamp, or the philosopher's stone. Virginia, as a State, cannot declare war, nor raise an army, nor maintain a navy, nor coin a copper cent or a silver dime, nor establish a post office, nor lay an import or export duty, nor make bank notes a legal tender, nor suspend the habeas corpus, nor abolish the trial by jury, nor ordain an established religion, nor make a treaty, nor enter into an alliance or confederation, nor pass an *ex post facto* law, or law impairing the obligation of contracts. All these things have been done, and may again of right be done, by absolutely sovereign States : but no State of the Union has ever exercised a single one of these sovereign prerogatives ; and, therefore, no State, after it became a member of the Union, can be said to be sovereign. To say, then, that the right of secession results from the sovereignty of the States—a quality which no separate State possesses—is an absurdity no less patent than that which supposes the Federal Government and that of the separate States to be each supreme within the same sphere. The doctrine is as void of reason as a barrel without heading is, of capacity to hold water.

But it is strenuously urged upon me, that when a State acts through a convention, her action then becomes the action of a sovereign State, and that my State, having in convention determined to secede, I and all her sons should follow in her track. I cannot recognise this logic. Undoubtedly, the action of a State, in convention, within the sphere of unquestioned authority, is the highest form her political action can assume. But if a thing is wrong under the higher law of the Federal Constitution, can a State make it right by doing it through the medium of a convention? Does the formality of a convention, any more than simple legislative proceeding, legalize that which is illegal? The Constitution says the laws of the Union shall be supreme: does the simple act of going into separate convention destroy that supremacy? The Constitution declares that not one of its provisions shall be changed, except by the concurrent assent of three-fourths of the States: does a State, by acting in convention, acquire the power, of itself, to change it? The constitution provides expressly that no State shall enter into any confederation or alliance: does the fact, that the Southern Confederacy was formed by the action of separate State conventions, invest that grand usurpation with constitutionality, and relieve the actors who set it up of the sin and wickedness of a deliberate infraction of an instrument, which they had in better times acknowledged to confer supreme authority, and which they had covenanted never to vary but by consultation with all the States, and the express sanction of a three-fourths majority of all? A State cannot declare war: can it acquire that forbidden power by seizing it in convention? Logically, the doctrine is absurd; and it is no better in morality: for it makes lawful, by a cheap and easy process, what was unlawful before; and, carried out, it negatives altogether the existence of a Confederated Government, and would make every Government of a Confederation but another name for anarchy, disruption, and revolution.

The naked truth is, then, that each State, the moment it assented to a Constitution which refers all matters of amendment to the tribunal of three-fourths of the States, renounced forever all right of separate secession, and in every form, whether of convention, or of ordinary legislation, or of direct vote of the people.

The renunciation was absolute and unconditional, without any limitation, qualification, or reservation.

This is the common sense view which entirely satisfies my conscience as to the position I have taken; but I am not a little comforted—in the midst of the contumely which my course has provoked at home—that it is sustained by the most eminent of State-rights authorities. Patrick Henry, the leading and most eloquent adversary of the Federal Constitution because of what he regarded its consolidation tendencies, early rebuked the idea of separate State secession. In the Virginia Convention, called in 1788, to consider the Federal Constitution, he said:

" Have they said, *We the States?* Have they made a proposal of a compact between *States?* If they *had*, this would be a Confederation : it is otherwise most clearly a *consolidated Government.* The whole question turns, sir, upon that poor little thing, the expression *We, the people*, instead of *the States*, of America."

And so, on the Hustings, in the county of Charlotte, lamenting the adoption by the Legislature of his State of the Resolutions of '98 as tending to Rebellion and Treason, he declared:

" That the State had quitted the sphere in which she had been placed by the Constitution ; and in daring to pronounce upon the validity of Federal laws, had gone out of her jurisdiction in a manner not warranted by any authority, and in the highest degree alarming to every considerate man ; that such opposition on the part of Virginia to the acts of the General Government, *must* beget their enforcement by military power ; that this would probably produce civil war ; civil war, foreign alliances ; and foreign alliances must necessarily end in subjugation to the powers called in."

How strangely and mournfully prophetic!

And on the same occasion, he put the whole doctrine of secession in a nutshell, and reduced it to a thrice-palpable absurdity by inquiring—

" *Whether the county of Charlotte would have authority to dispute an obedience to the laws of Virginia, and he pronounced Virginia to be to the Union, what the county of Charlotte was to her.*"

Mr. Jefferson, while the Virginia convention of 1788 was in session, complimented that admirable provision of the Federal Constitution (then under consideration in his State) which secured the peaceable recourse to a convention of the States. At a later day he said that, in the event of serious differences between the Federal Government and a State or States, "*which could neither be avoided nor compromised, a Convention of the States must* be called to ascribe the doubtful power to that department which they may think best."

John Taylor, of Caroline, the strictest State-rights politician Virginia ever reared, declared that—

" The supremacy over the Constitution was deposited in three-fourths of the States."

That provision he denominated as one—

" For settling collisions between the State and Federal Government amicably, and for avoiding dangerous sectional conflicts."

In 1833, Mr. Calhoun said:

" There is provided a power even over the Constitution itself, vested in three-fourths of the States, which Congress has the authority to invoke, and may terminate all controversies in reference to the subject, by granting or withholding the right in contest. Its authority is acknowledged by all, and to deny or resist it would be, on the part of the State, a violation of the constitutional compact, and a dissolution of the political association, as far as it is concerned. This is the ultimate and highest power, and the basis on which the whole system rests."

He even declared it to be the duty of the Federal Government to—

" Suppress physical force as an element of change."

And again, in 1843, when Secretary of State:

" Should the General Government and a State come into conflict, the power which called the General Government into existence, which gave it all its authority, and can enlarge, contract, or abolish its powers at its pleasure, may be invoked. The States themselves may be appealed to—three-fourths of which form a power whose decrees are the Constitution itself, and whose voice can silence all discontent.

" The utmost extent of the power is that a State, acting in its sovereign capacity as one of the parties to the constitutional compact, may compel the Government created by that compact to submit a question touching the infraction to the parties who created it."

Mr. Ritchie, the editor of the *Richmond Enquirer*, who for near half a century gave law to the State-rights Democracy of Virginia, if not of the Union, wrote, in 1814, as follows:

" No man, no association of men, no State or set of States has a right to withdraw from the Union of its own accord. The same power that knit us together can alone unknit. The same formality that forged the links of the Union, is necessary to dissolve it. The majority of States which form the Union, must consent to the withdrawal of any one branch of it. Until that consent has been obtained, any attempt to dissolve the Union, or obstruct the efficiency of its Constitutional laws, is treason—treason to all intents and purposes."

This logic of these distinguished representatives of the State-rights principle leads directly and irresistibly to this result—it is a manifest corollary—that so long as the Constitution of the United States remains unchanged by the constitutional majority of three-fourths of all the States, no one State has the right to secede; the

2

Union constitutionally endures; and, constitutionally enduring, it is obligatory, in each and every one of its provisions, on every citizen of every State of the Union.

With this truth stamped upon my understanding so that I could not resist it, I have not been able, in conscience, by taking an oath of exclusive allegiance to Virginia, to renounce that higher allegiance I owe to the Government of the Union. If I am in error, my own State, and her own State-rights teachers, indoctrinated me with the error.

And my conscience is eased yet the more when I bring to mind the fact, that nearly all the great minds of my State have set me the example of repudiating the doctrine, and denouncing it as treason. I know but one of the really great men of Virginia, that ever favored it, and that one was Littleton Waller Tazewell, a man, undoubtedly, of extraordinary abilities, but whose great powers, like those of Mr. Calhoun, were impaired by a metaphysical subtlety illy suited to the deduction of truth, and to successful dealing with the practical concerns of human government. Both wanted the practical common sense and well-balanced judgment which made Henry Clay the greatest statesman of his day, if not of any day or generation.

Mr. Tazewell did maintain the theory of constitutional separate State secession. In a series of articles over the signature of "A Virginian," published in the *Norfolk Herald*, he made for it the ablest argument it ever challenged, or that ever will be made for it by mortal intellect. But he stands almost "solitary and alone" in his glory. Neither Washington, nor Patrick Henry, nor Jefferson, nor Madison, nor Chief Justice Marshall, nor John Taylor, nor Spencer Roane, nor William Wirt, nor Philip Doddridge, nor Daniel Sheffey, nor Judge Robert B. Taylor, nor Geo. Keith Taylor, nor Geo. W. Summers, nor Judge John Scott, nor Judge Robert Stanard, nor Robert E. Scott, nor Alexander H. H. Stuart, concurred with him. These authorities will be regarded, I am sure, a full offset against the opinion of Mr. Tazewell, and on such authorities I am quite content to rest my defence for not following my State in her mad plunge into secession.

But there is one chapter in the political history of Virginia from which I must quote, because it contains, for us who could not abandon the Federal Union, a vindication which must tell upon all reasonable minds, and disarm our revilers.

In 1808, the Madison electors of Virginia met at a social dinner in Richmond. Judge Spencer Roane, then of the Court of Appeals, and the Nestor of the State-rights party of his State, presided. The electors came from all parts of the State, and were men of eminent ability and unsuspected State-rights republicanism. Some of those who participated were Whigs of the Revolution, fresh, comparatively, from its battle-fields, and its untainted halls of legislation. On this interesting occasion, a certain toast—not a volunteer, but a regular one—was drunk. What was it? It was nothing more nor less than this:

"*The Union of the States: the majority must govern; it is treason to secede.*"

Now, according to these sentiments of the Madisonian era, am I a traitor to my State because I cannot follow her into disunion, and ought I to be asked to take to her an oath of exclusive allegiance?

From another chapter of Virginia history, I must quote to set right a most remarkable error bearing on our subject.

The next ablest argument for secession to Mr. Tazewell's, is one made some 18 months since by Judge Allen, of the Court of Appeals of Virginia, which has done much, more than all others, perhaps, to diffuse through the body politic of his State the poison of secession.

But the whole force of his argument rests upon a fallacy, the exposure of which utterly annihilates his reasoning.

The fallacy is this: The Virginia Convention for ratifying the Federal Constitution, adopted the following form of ratification:

"We, the delegates of the people of Virginia, &c., &c., do, in the name and in behalf of the people of Virginia, declare and make known, that the 'powers granted under the Constitution, *being derived from the people of the United States, may be resumed* BY THEM whensoever the same shall be perverted to their injury or oppression.' "

The expression "the people of the United States," is construed by Judge Allen to mean the people of *the States separately*, whereas it is manifest that the people of the States *as a Union— as a Confederation—as a Government—as a nation—as the people of so many States as formed the Union, and could lawfully change it*, were meant. For the powers granted under the Constitution were not granted by a single, separate State, *but by a given number of States.* Not one State, nor two States, could grant the powers, and if any one State—to illustrate the absurdity of the theory—could resume the granted powers, any other one State could do the like, and so the Federal Government, though designed to "form a more perfect Union," and to "secure the blessings of liberty to ourselves *and our posterity,*" would be the merest rope of sand.

Nobody doubts that the constitutional majority of three-fourths of the States may change the form of the Government—may even let a particular State out of the Union; but that any one State may let itself out, and resume the powers originally granted, not by one State, but by a number of States, is altogether a different proposition, and one not to be tolerated on any sound theory of government, or sound principle of construction.

But, conceding Judge Allen's theory to be sound, it has no application to the present secession movement; for he does not show, nor has any man yet shown, that the powers granted by the people in the Federal Constitution have ever been "*perverted to their injury or oppression.*"

If I travel beyond Virginia, I find abundant accordance with the opinions of her own distinguished statesmen.

In South Carolina—the State that inaugurated the secession policy, and that, according to the confessions of her own chief public men, has been striving for more than thirty years to sever the Union—it was held by her Supreme Court that her citizens owe *primary* allegiance to the Government of the United States, and a *subordinate* one to their State. (Case of State *vs.* Hunt, 2 Hill's S. C. Reps., p. 1.)

In 1833, the State of Delaware, reprehending the mistaken action of South Carolina in attempting a severance of the Union on account of the tariff policy, maintained these catholic propositions:

"*Resolved by the Senate and House of Representatives of the State of Delaware in General Assembly met,* That the Constitution of the United States is *not a treaty* or compact between sovereign States, but a form of *government emanating from, and established by, the authority of the people of the United States of America.*

"*Resolved,* That the Government of the United States, although one of limited powers, is *Supreme* within its sphere, and that the *people of the United States owe to it an alle-

giance that cannot be withdrawn, either by individuals or masses of individuals, without its consent.

"*Resolved*, That the Supreme Court of the United States is the only and proper tribunal for the settlement, in the last resort, of controversies in relation to the Constitution and the laws of Congress."

Mississippi, too, among the most rampant and infatuated of the secession States, in 1851, in a convention of her people, adopted the following resolution :

"*Resolved*, That, in the opinion of this convention, the asserted right of secession from the Union, on the part of a State or States, *is utterly unsanctioned by the Federal Constitution*, which was framed to establish, and not to destroy, the Union of the States."

General Jackson said, in 1833 :

"Their object is disunion ; but be not deceived by names—disunion, by armed force, is treason."

Judge Iredell and Gov. Davie, of North Carolina, two of her most distinguished citizens, and Charles Cottsworth Pinckney, of South Carolina, bitterly disputed the right of secession.

And Hon. Howell Cobb, in 1851, used this language :

"When asked to concede the right of a State to secede at pleasure from the Union, with or without just cause, we are called upon to admit that the framers of the Constitution did that which was never done by any other people possessed of their good sense and intelligence—that is, to provide, in the very organization of the Government, for its dissolution. I have no hesitation in declaring that the convictions of my own judgment are well settled, that no such principle was contemplated in the adoption of our Constitution."

And to come, lastly, to that highest and most conclusive authority, to which all good citizens bow in unreluctant acquiescence, the Supreme Court of the United States has forever settled the unconstitutionality of secession.

In the case of Cohens *vs.* Virginia, Chief Justice Marshall, in delivering the opinion of the court, ruled as follows :

"The people made the Constitution, and the people can unmake it. It is the creature of their will, and lives only by the r will. But this supreme and irresistible power to make or unmake resides in the whole body of the people, *and not in any subdivision of them. The attempt of any of the parts to exercise it is usurpation, and ought to be repelled by those to whom the people have delegated their power of repelling it.*"

Here, on this broad, firm ground—the adjudication of the highest judicial tribunal of my country—I stand, and on it, so help me God, I mean to stand while I live. If I did not stand content on this rock of defiant safety, and from its proud summit laugh to scorn the impotent lashings of the angry waves beneath, I should be unworthy of the blessings of this great, free Government of ours; for the experience of all the world testifies that, after all, the safest reliance for human liberty, its most impregnable bulwark, is to be found in the judicial tribunals. Please tell my old friends who think me traitor for not going with my State, and who wish me to take an oath of allegiance to her, separately, and to the Southern Confederacy, collectively, that the Supreme Court of the United States, John Marshall being Chief Justice, tell me that if I comply I shall do an unconstitutional, unlawful, wicked act, and that, therefore, I cannot and will not do it.

The truth is, our State has been so capricious in her political rulings, that her citizens may well halt before following her blindly. In 1798, she planted herself on the position that the Federal Government should not be resisted except in case of "deliberate, palpable, and dangerous infractions of the Constitution." Obeying this her ancient ruling, I cannot go with her into secession, for I know of no "deliberate, palpable, and dangerous infraction" of her constitutional rights. The Federal Government has never done her a wrong that I know of, of any kind. In 1849, she declared, by legislative resolves, that if Congress should abolish slavery in the District of Columbia, or interfere with the slave trade between the States, or with slavery within the States, or apply the Wilmot proviso to the common territories, she would "resist at all hazards and to the last extremity." But not one of these things has been done by Congress. And so, in 1851, she approved by an unanimous vote of her General Assembly that measure of peace and concord, the Compromise of 1850; and now, alas! without the commission of any fresh outrage by the Federal Government or the people of the north, save the election of the man of their choice to the Presidency, she allows herself to be dragged over the precipice of disunion!

What, in this conflict of her own positions, must I do? Must I be dragged along with her? No—I cannot: I must, as a citizen, judge for myself, and follow whither conscience and duty lead.

Will I, then, never go with my State, as I have been often

asked by my disunion friends? Are there no circumstances under which I would have her secede? Will I be always a submissionist?

I answer: there *are* circumstances under which I would follow my State "at all hazards and to the last extremity." When she is right in her resistance—when she is grievously and insufferably wronged and oppressed—when she is so clearly in the right that I can feel conscious that the God of battles will be with her in her fight—then I will go with her and die for her, but not before.

A certain great man—one of the most distinguished of men—*clarum et venerabile nomen*—a man whom I loved and admired while living, and whose memory I fondly reverence—the first statesman of his day—among the wisest the world ever saw—the noblest, most unselfish, most disinterested, of patriots—whose rank was with Madison, and Lowndes, and Canning, and Pitt, and Peel,—who was one of the "bright particular" ornaments, not of his country only, but of the world: a countryman of ours answering faithfully this description, once used the following language:

" I have heard with pain and regret a confirmation of the remark I made, that the sentiment of disunion is becoming familiar. I hope it is confined to South Carolina. I do not regard as my duty what the honorable Senator seems to regard as his. If Kentucky to-morrow unfurls the banner of resistance, unjustly, I will never fight under that banner. I owe a paramount allegiance to the whole Union—a subordinate one to my own State. *When my State is right—when she has cause for resistance—when tyranny and wrong, and oppression insufferable arise—I will share her fortunes. But if she summons me to the battle field, or to support her in any cause that is unjust against the Union, never, never will I engage with her in such a cause.*"

The author of these admirable sentiments was the author of that other immortal one, "I had rather be right than be President."—Henry Clay.

Now, when any of my old line, Henry Clay Whig friends at home—you were one—should ask when it is that I will go with my State, let them be referred to these sentiments of Mr. Clay, and from them receive my answer. Let them be told that, in my best judgment, the State is *not right* in taking the part she has in secession—"that tyranny, wrong, and oppression insufferable" have *not* yet arisen—that she has no more cause of complaint now than she had in 1851, when she virtually endorsed these opinions of the great Kentuckian by approving and accepting the compromise measures of 1850 as a "full and final settlement of all the agitating questions to which they related," and that, accordingly, a state of things exists which subordinates the allegiance I owe the State to that higher "paramount allegiance which I owe the whole Union."

But it is urged upon me, again, that if the secession of the Southern States finds no warrant in the Constitution, it *has* warrant in the law of Revolution.

This is a clear change of the issue. Not one of the seceding States rested its action on the right of Revolution. All appealed to the high pretension that to secede was matter of right—of *magna charta*—of Constitutional privilege—of reserved right, overcoming all the express provisions of the National Constitution. But change the issue to Revolution, and a yet flimsier pretext is substituted.

The right of Revolution is not an arbitrary thing. It is a principle; and a principle, too, of the utmost consequence in the great practical concerns of mankind. Men associated in a society may not at will throw off its trammels, otherwise the peace of the community would never be safe. Disorder, civil commotion, violence, bloodshed and war, would stand ever ready for the beckon of the vicious and the desperate. There would be no stability in the rights of property, or of any of the personal rights. There would be no repose for innocent and helpless women and children, and other non-combatants of society. Society, indeed, would be but a series of commotions and desolations. Revolution, then, being a principle, what is the principle? It is philosophically and beautifully illustrated in the celebrated lines of Shakespeare, "rather endure those ills we have, than fly to others that we know not of," and it is this: that existing arrangements of society and government are not to be disturbed to the extent of force and war, unless on the ground of grievous wrong or intolerable oppression. When these arise, it is the great privilege of man, as it is his great instinct, to rise up in all his majesty and might, and resist even unto war, blood, and death.

This being the principle, it has no application to, and is no justification for, the dismemberment of the Union by the seceded States.

On the day of the Presidential election, in November, 1860, from which period the active movements towards secession date, the country was never in a more prosperous condition, or its people happier. The effects of the commercial revulsion of 1857 had almost disappeared under the recuperating agency of bountiful crops; and peace, plenty, and content, reigned through the land. This state of prosperity and repose was disturbed for no adequate cause. In my judgment, we have been precipitated into civil war, with all its revolting incidents of social and physical desolation, *without any cause at all*. I lament to say it; but it is true, that this whole secession movement is nothing more nor less than downright rebellion, and rebellion against the best and the most parental Government that ever a people had.

In Virginia, it is complained that great outrages have been committed on southern rights. By whom? Certainly not by the Federal Government, of whose action alone is there any danger. If any outrages have been perpetrated, what are they? I know them not; no, not one. I frequently appealed to the leading secessionists of Virginia, while there, both in public and private, in the legislative halls, on the hustings, at the cross-streets and the cross-roads, to name to me one wrong which the Government they were so anxious to subvert, had ever done the south, and I was never answered by any specification. I heard, ever and anon, some indefinite grumbling about the Wilmot Proviso, and Personal Liberty laws, and interference with the rights of slaveholders; but I never met the first man who could point his finger to the first act of actual aggression by the Federal Government upon the rights of the south.

So far from the commission of any positive aggression, I must say, and do say, that the course of the Federal Government—of Congress, the only practical representative of that Government and the people—has been everything the south could ask. First, on the demand of the south, Congress enacted, not one, but two fugitive slave laws. The first did not suit, and a better one was asked for and obtained. The south assented, almost unanimously, to the Missouri Compromise; but, becoming dissatisfied with it,

3

asked for the obliteration of the geographical line between slavery and freedom, and Congress hearkened to the demand, the peculiar northern friends of the south, in Congress and out of it, sustaining the repeal of the Missouri Compromise. The south protested against the application of the Wilmot Proviso to the common territories, and Congress listened. No law applying the Wilmot proviso has been enacted. On the contrary, several territorial laws, embracing the whole disposable territory of the United States, have been passed, which contained no prohibition as to slavery. And now any citizen is free to go to any of the territories with his slaves, if he chooses, unmolested by any action of the Federal Government, and with all the protection open to him which the courts can give to his rights of property. The south complained of the Personal Liberty statutes of the north, for which the Federal Government is not responsible; and yet what did Congress do, in this regard? To quiet the apprehensions of the southern people, and to preserve the national quiet, it did all it could do—*it passed by a vote of* 151 *to* 14—*almost unanimous—a resolution, recommending to the northern States the repeal of their Personal Liberty laws;* and there can be no doubt, that if the south had not precipitated itself into secession, this patriotic and friendly recommendation of the people's representatives would have had its effect in the repeal of most, if not all, the offensive statutes. The south expressed its apprehension—for which there never was any just ground—that slavery in the States would be assailed, and said new guarantees were wanted, when Congress, by a vote almost unanimous, adopted the following resolutions :

" *Resolved,* That neither the Federal Government nor the people or governments of the non-slaveholding States have a purpose or a constitutional right to legislate upon, or interfere with, slavery in any of the States of the Union.

Resolved, That those persons in the north who do not subscribe to the foregoing proposition are too insignificant in numbers and influence to excite the serious attention or alarm of any portion of the people of the Republic, and that the increase of their numbers and influence does not keep pace with the increase of the aggregate population of the Union."

It went still further—did all that any reasonable man in the south could have asked : by the necessary constitutional majority, it recommended to the States *the adoption of an amendment to the*

Constitution (proposed, I think, by Mr. Seward) *which should forever forbid the interference by Congress with slavery in the States.* [This proposition was voted against by Mr. Toombs and Mr. Davis.] And when John Brown's invasion of Virginia was denounced as a great outrage, to prevent the repetition of the like raids, it was proposed in the Senate Compromise Committee, by Mr. Seward, to pass a law to punish all persons hereafter making such invasion, and though voted for by all the northern members of the committee, the proposition failed for want of the co-operation of the southern members.

As to the absorbing matter of slavery, then, let us see how the case stands, or how it might have stood, had the seceding States been a little more patient. The proposed amendment to prohibit forever all interference with slavery, had been, early after the election of Mr. Lincoln, submitted by Congress to the States. The legislatures of three-fourths of the States, or the people of three-fourths of the States in convention, might have adopted it, and thus made it a part of the Constitution. Had all the slave States adopted it, there is no doubt a sufficient number of the free States would have co-operated to secure the constitutional majority of three-fourths, and then what would have been the result? Why, that would have been accomplished for which the whole south had professed to be so anxious—*Slavery in the States would have been perpetually protected ; the agitation of the long-disturbing question would have ceased, except with a few demented fanatics ; and the concord of former days would have been restored.*

Slavery in the States being thus rendered impregnable, there would have been nothing left of this subject to disturb the national harmony but the territorial question, and that is of no practical moment, for there is not a foot of the present Territories that is adapted to slave labor, or to which slave labor could profitably go. In New Mexico, for example, five times as large as New York, there are but twenty-six slaves, (who are the body servants of Government and Army officers,) though slavery is there legal, and protected by a slave code. Of what practical consequence to the south, then, is the right of carrying slaves to Territories from which the God of nature, by His laws of soil and climate, and by the instincts He has planted in man, has forever excluded them ? And why should the north care to prohibit slavery in Territories, into which, for the inhibitions named, it can never be introduced?

In fact, all that the south can properly demand in regard to slavery in the Territories, as Judge Campbell, late of the Supreme Court, contended, is, that the *status quo* be observed. I quote his wise and patriotic words, addressed to the people of Alabama:

" The great subject of disturbance—that of slavery in the Territories—rests upon a satisfactory foundation, and we have nothing to ask, except that the *status quo* be respected."

Well, the *status quo* HAS been respected—I think, scrupulously respected. Notwithstanding the repeal of the Missouri Compromise, which so much and so justly offended northern sensibilities, and in defiance of the outside pressure which the repeal of that measure of plighted faith and honor generated, Congress has not applied the Wilmot Proviso to any of the Territories. It has wisely left the matter to the laws of God—of soil, production, climate, and profit—and to the courts, to which the whole subject so properly belongs.

Now, with the promise of perpetual guarantees for slavery in the States, and the observance of the *status quo* as to the Territories, what reason was there that Virginia and her deluded sisters should have seceded from our blessed Union?

I thought, as I still think, that all the slave States should have submitted the amendment of the Constitution forbidding future interference with slavery in the States, to their Legislatures or people, and obtained in that way the security desired for their peculiar institution. Then, instead of the civil war whose demon howl now rings through the land, and whose desolation is carried to the hearth, and the fire-side, and every relation and interest of life, we should have continued to realize that peace and happiness, which, under our glorious institutions, have blessed us above all the people of the earth. Oh! what a chance did we lose of saving our country and ourselves! How mad was it, with so cheering a prospect for the happy solution of all our difficulties, to plunge into the gulf of ruin forever!

And why, let me ask, did we *not* make the effort for peace and salvation? Alas! I fear there was a foregone conclusion to destroy the Union, without regard to wrongs, or the remedies for them! What does the refusal of the south to accept Mr. Seward's amendment indicate but that no compromise was desired, and that disunion was resolved on, under any and all circumstances? Why was not the north met half-way, in proposals for peace and guarantees?

And, at the time of Mr. Lincoln's election, what semblance of danger was there to the south? There was a clear opposition majority of 21 in the House of Representatives, and a conclusive one in the Senate. How, under such circumstances, could the south have been harmed? Could slavery have been abolished in the District of Columbia? Could it have been prohibited in the Territories? Could it have been touched in the States? Was it possible that Mr. Lincoln could have harmed the south a hair's breadth, even had he the disposition?

Besides having both branches of Congress on its side, had not the south the Supreme Court? Had not the decisions of that high tribunal leaned to the side of slavery and slave holders? And had not Congress, in the several territorial laws, referred all rights of property—slave and other—to that august and trustworthy tribunal?

Then, the fact is simply this: that with an entire absence of all aggressive legislation, the south had the Legislature and Judiciary to itself. Only the Executive was against it, or was supposed to be against it, and that branch was impotent for harm, because an inimical measure could never reach it. The south, indeed, had every thing its own way, was as impregnable as a well-equipped army behind a strong entrenchment would be from the outside assaults of a few ragged regiments, armed with pop guns—and yet the south, with horse-leech avidity, cried: "Give us more, or we will dash the Union into fragments!"

Surely the history of mankind affords no parallel to this remarkable infatuation! It stands alone. There has never been before so impious a defiance of the goodness of the Creator—such a sporting with the beneficence of Providence—so mad a case of self-ruin and self-destruction!

My own deep belief is, that those who busied themselves in this great wickedness, will never be able to account to the Christian world for their participation in it. How I thank God that I have had no part nor lot in the matter! And as each sand of the unhappy conflict runs out, the more thankful am I, that I had the firmness to repudiate and reject all the projects of the secessionists!

The proposition so often submitted to me that Mr. Lincoln's election is adequate cause for a dissolution of the Union, I look upon with absolute horror. The doctrine that the election by a legal majority of the people of the President of their choice is a sufficient reason for the dissolution of the Union, is so monstrous, so antagonistical to all the theory and maxims of popular and Republican Government, so replete with radicalism and lawlessness, so perilous to all the vested interests of society, so fraught with moral and social chaos and ruin, so barbarous, that I dismiss it, once and forever, with my utter and eternal abhorrence. I will not even quote against it the authority of the great men of the south, of all parties, who have repudiated the detestable heresy. Its own blackness is its own best exponent!

And the folly of secession—of resorting to the cartridge-box instead of the ballot-box, for redress—is more apparent still, when we look at the presidential vote of 1860.

The whole opposition vote was 2,804,000; the Republican vote 1,857,000: majority against the Republicans, nearly a million. Now, with this million conservative pro-southern majority, would it not have been far wiser (as I argued on another occasion) to have made another trial of strength before throwing aside the best Government the world ever saw? Is not a quiet victory at the polls preferable to a revolution, in which the sword must decide the issue? Should we have precipitated disunion by four years for a danger which was that length of time distant, at least, and which, by the end of that period, might have vanished altogether, by a change in the political sentiment of the country? Should we, for an imaginary peril, have taken disunion four whole years by the forelock? Was the Union of so little value that we should absolutely have made haste to destroy it—to kill it off before its time had come?

To the idea that the election of Mr. Lincoln evinced a sectionalism and hostility at the north, which would endanger the institution of slavery, it is sufficient to reply that the facts show it to be utterly unsound.

In a Union Address to my late constituents, published in January, 1861, I used the following language:

" Perhaps, no presidential vote was ever cast that was more complex in its character than that which was cast in November last. There were scores upon scores of thousands, even of the democracy, that were bitter in their hostility to Mr. Buchanan's Administration. Large numbers regarded it as corrupt; for corruption had been charged from high democratic sources. Hon. Roger A. Pryor was among the foremost in this denunciation. The Lecompton policy had lost to the Administration, and driven over to the Republican ranks, an army of its former friends. The financial policy of the Government, based on constant loans and issues of treasury notes, instead of duties on imports under a properly regulated tariff, turned the attention of a large number of people of the north to a change of Administration. Pennsylvania, always conservative until, desperate for the proper governmental appreciation of her material interests, she was compelled to take sides with the candidate most likely to succeed. (who was undoubtedly Mr. Lincoln,) cast her vote, mainly, on the tariff question. Now, all these classes of voters, numbering, it must be, several hundreds of thousands, desired a change of administration, and very naturally looked to the most available nominee, and regarding Mr. Lincoln, in consequence of the hopeless divisions of the democracy, as that most available nominee, cast their votes for him, without meaning to endorse his peculiar views on the subject of slavery. Disunion, then, on the idea of an irreconcilable northern enmity to southern institutions, rests upon an assumption unsound, unsubstantial, and suicidal."

And thus is annihilated another favorite pretext of the disunionists.

As for the Personal Liberty laws, no one ever lost a slave by them. Mostly, they are mere anti-kidnapping statutes, and whether constitutional or not, they should be to the south matter of indifference. Nor have all the free States passed such laws. Neither New York, nor Ohio, nor Minnesota, nor Iowa, nor Illinois, nor Indiana, nor New Jersey, has one. In Indiana and Illinois, slaves are arrested without process and returned to their masters. The wives of Kentuckians go into those States on social visits, with their colored domestics, unattended by their husbands. These facts I have heretofore publicly stated, on the authority of letters addressed to myself by Hon. Robert Mallory and W. R. Kinney, esq., of Kentucky, who reside on or near the Ohio river. Illinois has a statute which allows slaves to stay with their masters sixty days within her territory; and New Jersey not only allows the transit of slaves with their masters, but has a fugitive slave law of her own, to aid in the execution of the Federal law of the same kind. But should we, for these practically harmless personal liberty statutes, destroy our glorious Union? I would not, if every northern statute book were half filled with them. No : I will stand yet by the Union of our fathers, trusting that the "sober second thought," and the prevalence of that feeling which, "in the times that tried men's souls," put Massachusetts "shoulder to shoulder" with Virginia, will strike from the statute books all these irritating enactments, believing as well as hoping, that the patriotic recommendation of the representatives of the people in the House of Commons of the nation, already referred to, will lead to that "consummation so devoutly to be wished." Some of them, indeed, have already been repealed.

But are we of the south ourselves without reproach in the matter of the enactment of offensive laws ? I regret to say, and I say it with a sense of shame, that the law of South Carolina in regard to colored seamen—the State that stands in the front rank, and that is the guiltiest of the guilty in this enormous wickedness of secession—is just as offensive, as violative of the great principles of civil liberty, as repugnant to the spirit and the letter of our Constitution, as the worst personal liberty law of the northern States. The constitutionality of this law South Carolina would not allow even to be considered in her courts, though Massachusetts deputed thither one of her most distinguished jurists, [Judge Hoar,] to test its validity.

For one, I act in this matter on the law of offset. Both sections have done wrong, and I let the misdoing of the one stand against the misdoing of the other, and let the Union rise up in all its lustrous glory between both, to rebuke the sectional spirit that would stand between it, and the accomplishment of the grand destiny of popular institutions in America.

With regard to the Fugitive Slave law—that fruitful source of agitation both north and south, and I might add of misapprehension—it is enough to say that it has been executed, with all reasonable fidelity and success. The idea generally prevailing in the south that the law was never executed, and fugitive slaves never returned, is entirely erroneous. Many are quietly surrendered whose cases are never heard of; only those cases reach the public in which there is some tumult, or in those rare instances in which wicked people resist the execution of the law, and which, therefore, make a noise in the newspapers, and furnish material for declamation on the stump, and in the bar-rooms. These latter instances are the exceptions, not the general rule. But for the tediousness of the detail, I could furnish almost a volume of examples of the successful execution of the law. The grand jury of the northern district of Ohio indicted seven persons for resisting the marshal, and I believe they were all found guilty, and punished with fine and imprisonment. A clergyman was convicted in Ohio of the same offense, and sentenced to an imprisonment of six months, and a fine of $1,500. There are several persons now in jail at Chicago who were convicted in an Illinois court by an Illinois jury for assisting in the rescue of a fugitive slave, and who were fined $1,500 each, for the non-payment of which they are now suffering the pains of a dreary imprisonment. Less than a year ago I remember that several slaves were arrested in Cincinnati, and quietly restored to their masters; and a journal of that city declared at the time, that "during the preceding three years not a colored person arrested on a warrant of a United States commissioner, had been set free or escaped." Judge Douglas declared in the Senate that Judge McLean had always executed the law with scrupulous fidelity. The Supreme Court of Massachusetts, consisting of five Republican judges, unanimously pronounced the fugitive slave law constitutional, and "binding on the people of Massachusetts." Since the election of Mr. Lincoln, several fugitives were arrested in Chicago, examined before a United States' commissioner at Springfield, and remanded to their owners in St. Louis; and since this arrest and rendition, it is well known that large numbers of fugitive slaves, finding that the law is to be enforced under the present as under past administrations, have been flocking to Canada for an asylum; and even since the secession of the southern States, fugitives have been peaceably arrested in Ohio, Indiana, and Illinois, and delivered to their owners.

I deal with this subject practically, and on this point I quote again from the address already referred to :

"The question, then, comes up, (which I have well weighed and considered,) is there enough of grievance and of wrong in these personal liberty laws to induce disruption? Ought we, can we, for these dead statutes, and a few exceptional cases of escapes of fugitive slaves, forego the priceless, incalculable benefits of a Union which was the handiwork of Washington, and Franklin, and Madison, and Gerry, and Robert

Morris, and Governeur Morris, and Laurens, and Pinckney, and Hamilton, and which has made the people of the United States the freest, the happiest, and the greatest nation on the globe? If we do, the madness and the folly of the deed will be without a parallel in the annals of human weakness and folly.

" And another great, practical inquiry for the Southern slaveholder, is, *will secession remedy or alleviate this evil of the escape of his slaves?* No : it will aggravate the grievance a thousand fold. The Union dissolved, and with its dissolution the fugitive-slave law gone; the obligation for the surrender of fugitive slaves cancelled ; with more than a million and a half of friends turned into foes: with the fierce animosities and implacable enmities which have ever attended the disruption of once friendly and confederated States; with none, either in law or friendship, to intercept the fugitive in his flight to his great asylum in Canada; with Canada brought down to the very border line of the border slave States, so that the under-ground railroad will no longer be needed, and slaves have but to cross a boundary to be free : I say, in this state of things, under the mistaken policy of secession, we shall lose one hundred, perhaps one thousand slaves where we now lose one; our slave property will be worthless ; and the border slave States, however reluctantly, will be driven, 'dragged' to general emancipation, or to a ruinous sacrifice, perhaps utter loss, of their slave property. What will a slave be worth in Virginia, or Maryland, or Kentucky, or Missouri, when, to obtain his freedom, he has but to cross a river or a line?

"Then if we value our slave property, and would hinder the escape of our slaves into the free States, we had better adhere to the Union. In that Union, and there only, lies the safety of the Southern slaveholder."

Oh! had we not better have lost twice or thrice as many of our slaves as we usually have, than to have given up the peace, and quiet, and domestic happiness, and material comfort which we all enjoyed under the Union of our fathers ? Is the loss of a few slaves to the south to be put in computation with that loss of social happiness, and sacrifice of property and material prosperity ; with the desolated hearths and ruined homes; with the untold agony of heart and the millions of crushed hopes, and the countless sufferings of the innocent and helpless; with the distrust, hate, and alienation, that have followed in the track of this great delusion of secession? Before God and man I say it, I would have preferred to have had the loss of fugitive slaves quadrupled, yea, quintupled, rather than to have had taken from me the inestimable blessings of the Union.

And, after all, has not the loss by the escape of our slaves been greatly overrated ? Mr. Everett showed in his address at the Academy of Music in New York, and from the census returns, that, in 1850, the number of fugitive slaves from all the slave States was only $\frac{1}{30}$ of one per cent., and that in 1860 it was only $\frac{1}{50}$ of one per cent.—a loss, too insignificant to be thought of, in comparison with the priceless blessings of the Union! The loss to the drovers of cattle in Virginia, in every drive, is generally about 10 per cent., while to owners of slaves, by escapes, it is only $\frac{1}{30}$ of one per cent., and I do not doubt that the annual loss to the drovers of the State in getting their cattle to market, is of larger pecuniary amount than that of all the slaveholders of the State by the escape of fugitive slaves.

At all events, it is an unfortunate period to dissolve the Union on account of the loss of fugitive slaves, for the ratio of loss is regularly diminishing under the more efficient fugitive slave law of 1850, and an improved public sentiment, and, doubtless, it would have continued to diminish. By the census of 1860, it appears that in the border slave States one slave escaped to every 2,527, and in 1860, one to every 3,276; or, by Mr. Everett's figures, $\frac{1}{35}$ of one per cent. in 1850, and $\frac{1}{40}$ of one per cent. in 1860—a result which demonstrates that the people of the south were gradually, but surely, acquiring additional security for their peculiar property.

A few most remarkable results exhibited by the census returns, and I have done with this branch of the subject. I find that in 1860, Texas lost 16 slaves—one in every 11,274; Alabama 36—one in every 12,087; Florida 11—one in every 5,614; Georgia 23—one in every 20,096; Louisiana 46—one in every 7,228; and South Carolina 23—one in every 17,501;—while the border States lost as follows: Virginia one in every 4,195; Missouri one in every 1,161; Kentucky one in every 1,895; and Maryland one in every 758! These statistics show that, so far as fugitive slaves and fugitive slave laws are concerned, the cotton States have far too insignificant an interest to excuse them for trifling, as they have done, with the Union, and the interests of the border States. Think of it—Georgia losing only one slave in every 20,096, dragging Virginia out of the Union, who loses one in every 4,195; and South Carolina, losing one in every 17,501, dragging out Maryland, who loses one in every 758, and Kentucky, who loses one in every 1,895! Virginians lost their manhood when they submitted to be thus dragged. I cannot be one of the dragged.

And how mournfully do these statistics illustrate, to slaveholders, the consequences of secession!

Florida loses, in a year, eleven slaves; value, at $600 each, $6,600. Lest she incur a loss, by escaping slaves, of $6,600 a year, she gives up a Government which had expended one hundred millions in her behalf, and encounters a debt greater than the value of all her slaves together!

Texas loses 16 slaves; value, $9,600. For this insignificant loss, she sacrifices the priceless benefits of a Union to which she owes her very existence as a State, and under whose benign auspices she has advanced, with unexampled pace, to prosperity and consequence!

South Carolina and Georgia lose each 23 slaves, per year; value to each, $13,600. For this paltry sum—not the worth of a respectable mansion-house in Charleston or Savannah — each looses herself from a Government under which her peculiar industry prospered to the amount, annually, of hundreds of millions of dollars, and against which neither can truly charge a single act of unkindness!

But it is with our own State I have chiefly to do. What has secession done for Virginia, in reference to her property in slaves?

In 1860, she lost 117 slaves. To make the argument altogether favorable to secession, I put the aggregate value down at $100,000. Suppose that to be her annual loss under the Union, what has she gained by secession? Her share of the Confederate debt cannot, up to this date, be less than $60,000,000. On her own State account her expenditure cannot be short of $40,000,-000 more. If the war continues a year longer (which is next to certain) her entire debt, on account of it, must reach at least 150 millions.

So that, to save a loss, by fugitive slaves, of $100,000 per annum, she incurs a debt of 150 millions, the annual interest on which, at the Virginia rate of 7 per cent., is ten and a half millions of dollars!

That is to say, the people of Virginia, to avoid a loss or tax of $100,000 a year, are made to jump into one of ten and a half millions a year, an increase from a hundred thousand dollars, under secession, to ten and a half millions under the Union, and a sum which would pay for the annual loss, by fugitive slaves, for one hundred and five years; or which, in the form of yearly taxation, would be a blasting incubus upon the whole material prosperity of the State for generations to come, and, at the end of the war, would induce an utter depopulation of her domain, as the only escape from an unendurable taxation; or, regarding this war debt as so much principal, it would pay the annual loss, by fugitive slaves, for fifteen hundred years to come!

Taking an illustration nearer home, the little county of Elizabeth City—the smallest in the State—has lost, since the opening of the rebellion, at least 1,000 slaves, worth, by the usual average, $500,000. So that, in the effort of her misguided people to get greater security for slave property, they have lost more in six months than the whole State has in five, perhaps ten years past. I doubt whether this county has lost a thousand dollars' worth of fugitive slaves during the last twenty-five years of its existence under the Union, while in 200 days of secession's reign, it has lost half a million's amount. In this, the county of my residence, there were rich farmers who, before secession's inauguration, owned large numbers of slaves, but who now have not one left to black their boots, or saddle a horse for them. Let these men, the very foremost to denounce me for adhering to the Union, tell me now which works better for their slave property, the blessed Union of our wise and good fathers, or that miserable delusion and humbug, of modern secession and a Southern Confederacy.

Yet another home illustration. It may be safely computed that the border counties, and those contiguous to the lines of the Federal armies, have lost, by escapes, at least 25,000 slaves since the rebellion began. The value of these, at $500 each, is $12,-500,000. So that the State has lost, in the first six months of secession, more slave property than she could have lost in 125 years of government under the Union, had it existed so long.

Again: Virginia has, in round numbers, half a million of slaves. Before secession came along, slaves were of great value. A likely field-hand commanded, readily, from 1,500 to 2,000 dollars. Good-looking children of seven or eight years' age, were worth almost as much as adults. Even old men and women brought large prices. It is safe to put the average value at $700 per head, which gives a total value of $350,000,000. And it is certainly safe to estimate the depreciation at one half each. So that, to escape the small annual loss of $100,000, our State rushes, by the path of secession, into an almost instant loss of one hundred and seventy-five millions!

Or, to illustrate for the whole Southern Confederacy, take the whole number of fugitive slaves in all the seceded States together. That number, according to the census of 1860, was only 458; value, at rate above, $320,600. The Confederate States' debt, contracted by secession, cannot be less than 500 millions of dollars. Then the seceded States, in order to shun an annual loss of $320,600, find themselves involved, in a twelve month, in a consuming debt of five hundred millions—a sum equal to one-third the value of all the slaves in all the seceded States together.

Let the account be stated:

Loss of the seceded States under a year of the Union, 458 slaves; cash value, $320,600:

Public debt accruing by reason of secession, and in a single year, $500,000,000:

From the secession debt of $500,000,000 take the Union loss of $320,600, and there is a balance in favor of the Union of $499,-680,000! This latter sum would have been the saving to the seceded States, had they remained in the Union, or, what is the same thing, the amount they have lost by going out of the Union.

One more, and the last illustration on this head; and it is one that must stamp absurdity and madness on the measure of secession forever.

By the census returns of 1860, it appears that the whole fifteen slave States lost, in that year, only 803 fugitive slaves. So effectual was the fugitive slave law of 1850, and so kind the spirit of the controlling masses at the north, that, in all the slaveholding States, only 803 slaves were fugitives in the period of a year. What was this loss, divided among fifteen States? At $500 each, it was only $401,500; at $700 each, it was only $562,500; at $1,000 each, it was only $803,100. Now, I ask, can any sane, practical, common-sense man, for either of these sums, give in exchange the priceless and countless blessings and glories of a

Union which sent protection, security, peace, quiet, plenty, gladness, and joy, to the hearths and fire-sides of every American citizen, north and south, east and west, wherever born or wherever living? Compared with this protection, and security, and peace, and quiet, and plenty, and gladness, and joy, how inexpressibly paltry are the eight hundred and three thousand one hundred dollars of loss by runaway slaves! For such a Union—for so vast and matchless a good—who would begrudge so small a premium, especially when the price is not extorted from us by wrongful authority, or for intentional oppression, but is the inseparable, uncontrollable result of the peculiar characteristics and condition and relations of the negro race?

And how much have we not exaggerated this whole matter of our loss of slave property! Only 458 slaves lost, in a year, by the eleven seceded, and 803 by the whole fifteen, of the slave-holding States! Many people in the south doubtless suppose that many thousands annually escape, and put down the southern loss at many millions every year, and this mis-information, I doubt not—indeed, I know it—has tended greatly to aggravate southern sensibility and excitement about slaves and slavery. But the census of '60 discloses the fact that, after all the angry dissensions, and sectional discord, and revolutionary commotion on account of the slavery question, the eleven seceded States lost, in twelve months, only 458 fugitive slaves, worth a little more than a quarter of a million of dollars, while all the slaveholding States together lost only 803, worth but about half a million!

If the southern mind had been properly informed on the statistics of the subject, I cannot believe that the fatal step of secession would ever have been ventured. But alas! political agitation, ambition, selfishness, and passion, have held before the people a thick veil which has hid from their vision the truths that so deeply concern them!

Contemplate the subject, then, in what aspect you will, secession has been blast and ruin to the slavery interests of Virginia, and of the entire south.

I do not mean to say that, in reference to existing disturbances, the people of the North are wholly faultless. The constant slavery agitation at the North, I concede, is properly offensive to the south. It is wrong, and I should be glad to see our northern brethren desisting from that which can have no effect but to irritate, and to weaken the chords that bind us to a common Government. But we of the south are not altogether without sin in the premises, for we ourselves have indulged in the largest liberty in the discussion of the slavery question, I have ever thought, to the detriment of the slaveholding interest, though Senator Hammond and Mr. Stephens, and some other prominent southern men assert, that "slavery has been greatly strengthened and fortified by agitation," and that "happy results for the south have come of the Abolition discussion." If the latter opinion be sound, the south had no cause of complaint, and certainly no need of upsetting the Union because of the anti-slavery discussion. Besides, this anti-slavery discussion has been going on for long years past, and if such discussion furnished just cause for a dissolution of the Union, it should have been dissolved long ago. But we did not, on this account, proceed to disruption under past Administrations. Why should we do it under Mr. Lincoln's? Is the anti-slavery agitation any worse under Mr. Lincoln's Administration than it was under Mr. Fillmore's, or Mr. Polk's, or Mr. Pierce's, or Mr. Buchanan's?

Verily, I must have far stronger reasons than this for surrendering the thousand blessings of the American Union. Were I to advocate its destruction on so unsubstantial a pretext—for it does not rise to the dignity of a reason—I should commit a crime against humanity I could never expiate, and for which I should deserve never to be forgiven by the Christian world.

No: *I will not*, because a few mad fanatics desecrate the pulpit and the hustings by Abolition ravings, give up the unrivaled blessings of the best Government on earth. These deluded and wicked men do not represent the mass of the northern people. When they shall, or when the Federal Government shall practically assail the institution of slavery, it will be quite time enough to think of disunion, as a remedy against anti-slavery operations.

You will see, from the views I have expressed to you, that all along I have taken a practical view of all the questions connected with this deplorable conflict. I have sought to take counsel of judgment rather than of passion, and the farther the conflict progresses, alas! how painfully am I reminded that I have chosen the wiser part! I have had constantly in my mind, and there to the end they will be kept and cherished, those remarkable sentiments of wisdom expressed by Judge Campbell to his fellow-citizens of Alabama, which should be written in letters of living light over the lintel of every American door: "IN MY OPINION, SEP-ARATE STATE ACTION WILL RESULT IN THE DIS-CREDIT AND DEFEAT OF EVERY MEASURE FOR REP-ARATION OR SECURITY."

There are yet other reasons why I could not follow our State into secession. Conceding that the citizen *is* bound by the action of his State, I am released from the obligation now, because I am not satisfied that the act of secession in Virginia is truly the act of her people. It was not the choice of her people. I lament to say it, but the proofs are overwhelming, that outside pressure, intimidation, coercion, misrepresentation, and sensation appeals, constantly made by the press and the politicians to the passions and prejudices of the multitude, forbade all freedom of thought and of action. Let us see.

The press and the politicians, with untiring effort, impressed it upon the masses that the Lincoln Government would not leave them the semblance of a right. Hence, it was the common popular expression, put into the mouths of the uninformed by designing disunionists—"we can't submit to a Black Republican Administration." And those who put this clap-trap argument upon the lips of the deceived, never took the care to tell the victims of their deception that there was a decided majority in both houses of Congress *against* the Black Republican Administration, and that that Administration was, therefore, powerless to harm the south.

The people were told, next, that they would be far better off with an independent southern republic than with the old Union, and that their taxes would be less, because then the south would no longer pay tribute to the north, and because there would be then no tariffs, but free trade, and direct trade, and cheap goods: appeals of all the most likely to delude the common mind.

Thirdly, it was represented, with ceaseless repetition, that if Virginia seceded, there would be no war—that her influence and

5

power were so great that the moment *she* seceded, all the border States would follow, and that then the Federal Government would "back down," and recognize the Southern Confederacy.

It was next strenuously urged that the northern people would not fight. Senator Hammond said in a public speech that the moment it should be announced that eight cotton States had seceded, "the north would grow pale and tremble, and revolution would be there, not here." And it was said, further, that, if it came to a fight, one southern man was equal to five northern. Then came the assurance that if the war began, foreign intervention would soon end it. France and England, it was hourly said, ever willing to weaken American power, would soon interfere, and, by recognising the Southern Confederacy, secure its independence, and give it peace.

And further to inveigle the people into secession, it was earnestly insisted that the democracy of the north were the natural allies, and had always been the friends, of the south, and that one-half of them would be on the side of the south, and that the north being thus divided and the south united, the latter would have its independence established without incurring any of the consequences of war.

Later in the struggle the secessionists mended their hold, and advanced to more passionate appeals. The people were told that the war was begun by Mr. Lincoln, and ·to subjugate the South.

Then, again, it was urged that the war, thus begun by Mr. Lincoln, and against the south, had for one of its objects the abolition of slavery.

And lastly, with a vehemence amounting to phrensy, the alarm was rung night and day, that Mr. Lincoln's proclamation of April 15, '61, was an out and out, actual declaration of war against the southern people, and an invasion of their homes.

These artful and passionate appeals so fired the popular mind, and so stimulated coercion and intimidation that a popular convention was called to assemble at Richmond, (I think on the 15th of April,) for the purpose, it was generally supposed, and as I solemnly believe, to drive the constitutional Convention (then sitting) into the adoption of a secession ordinance.

The call of Mr. Lincoln for the militia to execute the laws, which, as I have just said, was proclaimed and denounced, with demoniac excitement, as an actual and deliberate declaration of war against the south, forestalled the purposed action of this popular convention, having produced the result designed, the passage of a secession ordinance, which took place on the 17th of April.

From the passage of the secession ordinance, to the 23d of May, when the final vote of the people was taken on it, the sensation efforts waxed fiercer and more wrathful, misrepresentation was redoubled, and coercion employed in every form, and when the hour of voting came, it is useless to say it was not a free vote. Had it been an untrammeled vote—a vote uninfluenced by fear or misrepresentation—I believe most solemnly that, this hour, the people of Virginia, instead of suffering all the horrors of a fratricidal war, would be quietly enjoying the manifold blessings of the Union.

I hold, with all deference, that a vote of my State, cast under such circumstances, is not binding on me as one of her citizens. The misrepresentation alone, to say nothing of intimidation and other forms of coercion, rendered the vote a fraud upon the elective franchise, and fraud vitiates all transactions.

I claimed the right, as a citizen, to judge the truth or falsehood of the various allegations on which the people of my State were asked to do the grave act of pulling down the noble fabric of Union, which their fathers had reared. I did judge, and my judgment was and is, that the allegations had no foundation in truth and fact.

I did not believe in the wrongs to the south which had been charged upon the north. I saw no practical aggression by the Federal Government upon the rights of the south. I asked "where are they?" and echo answered, "where are they?" I did not believe that secession could avert war. I did not believe in peaceable secession. With the great Webster, I did not believe in the "breaking up of the fountains of the great deep without ruffling the surface." I did not believe in, or dread foreign intervention. I believed the north *would* fight. I did not believe that the democracy of the north and west would fight for the south against the old flag. I knew, full well, that whenever traitorous hands should dare haul down the nation's star-gemmed banner, "the great Bell Roland" would toll, and millions would rush from city, country, valley, and mountain, to fling back its glory-lit folds to the breeze. I did not believe, nor do I now, that the Federal Government began the war, nor can any man, who has the least regard for truth, so say. The war was begun when South Carolina, by secession, broke equally her own .faith, and the laws of the United States.

The war advanced as each other State successively seceded. The war was palpable and unmistakable, and aggressive and wicked, when the forts, ships, arms, mints, and money of the United States, were forcibly seized by the seceding States. If the forcible seizure of forts and ships, and arms and mints, does not constitute war, in God's name what does? Did not war flame when the Confederate States opened their batteries upon Fort Sumter, confessedly the property of the United States? What is war but a hostile assault by one nation upon another? And who, in this conflict, made the first assault?

Nor do I believe that Mr. Lincoln's proclamation was war upon Virginia, or the south. And as this proclamation was most successfully wielded for inflaming the popular mind, and did more than all else, perhaps, to induce the secession of Virginia, I note the point especially.

The proclamation was war upon nobody. It was *defence against war*. Nay, more, it was duty. The President of the United States would have been false to duty and to honor, if, after the bombardment of Fort Sumter, he had failed to call out the militia. I think he should have done so the first moment after his inauguration; for he found, on his accession, several States by force resisting the laws of the United States, in actual possession of United States forts, and, indeed, in actual, undoubtful rebellion. Mr. Buchanan had virtually abdicated the Government, and surrendered to the open violators of the laws and the avowed enemies of the Government, and Mr. Lincoln would have been entirely right if he had made the calling out of the militia the very first act of his Administration. In not doing so, he exhibited especial moderation, prompted, no doubt, by a patriotic desire for peaceful adjustment. In any event, he did only what Washington had done before him. Washington called out the militia to put down the whiskey insurrection in Pennsylvania, under the act of 1792; Mr. Lincoln called it out to suppress a far greater and more wicked rebellion, under the act of 1795, which was made more stringent than the act of '92, and of indefinite duration, whereas the act of '92 was limited to less than three years. These modifications were doubtless suggested by the Pennsylvania rebellion. At all events, there was the law—declared by the Supreme Court to be constitutional—in full force; there it was, staring Mr. Lincoln in the face, and commanding him, "whenever the laws of the United States should be opposed, or the execution thereof be obstructed in any State, by combinations too powerful to be suppressed by the ordinary course of judicial proceedings, or by the powers vested in the marshals, to call forth the militia to suppress the combinations, and see the laws duly executed." Had he, with this statute before him, failed to call the militia into service, he would not only have been unfaithful to his trust, but the sin of perjury would have rested upon him. Nor could the pregnant facts have been overlooked or disregarded that, on the 6th of March—seven weeks anterior to the date of the Proclamation—the Congress of the Coneflerate States had made provision, by law, for raising an army of 100,000 men, and that the Secretary of War of the Confederate States had boasted, on the 12th of May—the day Fort Sumter was bombarded—"that the flag of the Confederate States of America would float over the dome of the Capitol at Washington before the first of July, and eventually over Fanueuil Hall itself." For what object was the raising of this large army provided for, but to resist the execution of the Federal laws within the seceded States?

The proclamation, then, of April the 15th, was no war upon Virginia.

No: Virginia herself commenced a war upon the United States. When the President called out the militia, he had the undoubted constitutional power to order their march at all times through the territory of Virginia, and of every other State. The Federal Government has, exclusively, the war-making power for the whole, Union, and the power to declare war and raise armies includes the power, necessarily, to march the federal troops all over the land. Had the militia then been marched into or through Virginia, it would have been no invasion of the "sacred soil." It would have been clear right, not a warlike act.

But which committed the first act of aggression, Virginia or the United States? The facts clearly put the responsibility on the former. As far back as the 30th of March, 1861—eighteen days before she seceded, and sixteen before the proclamation—Virginia had seized the United States guns at Bellona arsenal. This I know personally, for I was at the time, as you know, a member of the Legislature, and resisted the act as unlawful and shameful. On the 17th of April, 1861, by order of Governor Letcher, the channel of Elizabeth river was obstructed by the sinking of vessels loaded with granite, so that United States ships could not pass up to the Navy Yard at Gosport, nor merchantmen to Norfolk, in pursuit of legitimate commerce. On the 18th of April, a force was sent by Gov. Letcher to take possession of Harper's Ferry, when the Virginia forces fired on the United States soldiers, and killed two. April the 18th, the custom-house and post office at Richmond were seized, and about the same time the custom-house at Norfolk, and the navy yard at Gosport. Now, all these were acts of war, and they transpired before a United States soldier trod the soil of Virginia, or a gun was fired within hearing of her people. On the 17th of April, Gov. Letcher issued his proclamation calling on the people of Virginia to hold themselves in readiness to resist the Federal troops; and on the 24th of April the State became a member of the Southern Confederacy. By this act, she became a party to all the hostile acts of the Government of the Confederate States—the bombardment of Fort Sumter, the seizure of the forts and ships, and all other illegal and belligerent acts of the new Confederation. All this was before any advance of a Federal army into Virginia. No advance was made, indeed, until the 24th of May, when Alexandria was taken. Nor would a hostile Federal foot-print have impressed her soil unless she had herself first committed acts of aggression and war, and invited and allowed the armed enemies of the United States to make her territory the battle-ground for the resistance of the Federal authority, and the destruction of the Government itself. Indeed, except for the contribution of her rightful military quota, the President's Proclamation calling forth the militia, did not apply to Virginia, and could not, until she had placed herself in the same category with the rebellious, resisting States. She chose to bring herself within the scope of the Proclamation, and the act and the awful consequences are her own. Had she taken the position of Maryland, Kentucky, and Missouri, every one of her loyal citizens would have been within the saving protection of the United States.

With what reason, then, can it be said that Mr. Lincoln made war on Virginia, and invaded the homes of her people? And yet thousands of her citizens were hurried into disunion by the misguided notion, that they were acting on the defensive against an unconstitutional and aggressive war.

Not less absurd was the pretext that the object of the war was to subjugate the south. There was not one fact to justify such a declaration. The proclamation of April the 15th looked only to the execution of the laws, and the defence of the Capital from threatened sack; and, since, there has been no act of the Government bearing the faintest semblance of subjugation.

And as groundless was the charge that general emancipation was an object of the war; for the Republican platform itself expressly disclaims all right of Federal interference with the domestic affairs and institutions of the States; the House of Representatives, early in 1861, several months before Virginia seceded, almost unanimously denied the right or the purpose of the Federal Government to interfere with slavery in the States; and at the extra session in July last, that body, by all the votes but two—and those two of southern men—declared that the purpose of the war was not the abolition of slavery or the subjugation of the south, but the salvation of the Government, and the restoration of the Union. As for the Executive branch of the Government, it has done nothing thus far to encourage the idea either of emancipation or subjugation. What may occur hereafter, I, of course, cannot undertake to say; but if the action of Mr. Lincoln in overruling the proclamation of Gen. Fremont, and the sentiments of Secretary Caleb B. Smith, in his patriotic speech delivered in Rhode Island during the past summer, be any index to the future conduct of the Administration, the struggle we are engaged in will preserve the character, thus far exhibited, of an honest effort for the preservation of the Government, and the bringing back of the ancient Union.

I repeat, secession was never the act of Virginia. A large majority of the members of her Convention had been elected as Union men, and but ten days before the passage of the secession ordinance, the ill-omened measure had been voted down by a heavy vote. Now I hold that the enactment of a secession ordinance by men who had been elected and trusted by the people as Union men, was in violation of every principle of representative government and of good faith; was, indeed, a daring fraud upon the elective franchise, and an outrage upon the sovereign people. The judgment pronounced at the polls in February last, which filled the convention with Union-pledged members, stood the judgment of the people until reversed by the same tribunal that had originally entered it up, and until set aside in the same solemn mode. Nothing had occurred to justify the presumption of a change of the popular sentiment but the President's Proclamation, which every member of the convention well knew was in strict pursuance of law, and did not, as a hostile or coercive measure, embrace Virginia at the time of its issue, for then she had not seceded. What the reason was for this sudden and extraordinary shifting; whether the outside pressure, in the shape of panic or intimidation, reached the hall of the convention or not, I undertake not to say. But I do say that, for some cause or other, the men of that body, distinguished as many of them are, did not act up to the great duty of a great occasion. Secession, under such circumstances, bound no one.

True, a vote of the people did, soon after, ratify the ordinance of secession, but the knee-shaking of the leading men was soon communicated, as if by contagion, to the alarmed and credulous masses, and contributed materially to the result; and, besides, it has been already demonstrated that, in that vote, there was no freedom. There was, in it, in truth, no more of moral freedom, than there would be of physical liberty in a person bound, hand and foot, with massive chains, too strong for human strength to sever.

With these views, honestly entertained, you will perceive how difficult it must be with me to tread, even with my State, the

thorny path of secession. I could not, and thank God I did not
yield to the misrepresentation, prejudice, passion, and intimidation, which rendered her vote on her secession ordinance a nul-
lity, and I am quite willing to bear all the consequences, be they
what they may.

There are still other reasons why I could not favor secession.
I thought I saw, in disunion, the sure doom of the great southern
institution of slavery. I am now convinced that my evil auguries
are at least approaching fulfilment, and by the acts of the slaveholders themselves. None else could have shaken the founda-
tions of the institution. Before this thing of secession began, it
was reposing quietly and safely and acquiring strength, its antagonisms gradually compromising on account of the constantly in-
creasing demand for cotton, rice, sugar, and tobacco, which are
most naturally and successfully the products of slave labor. But
necessity is a shrewd teacher; and it is now discovered that many
regions of the earth hitherto regarded as unsuited to the cotton
culture, are well adapted to it. To say nothing of India and
Australia—Central America and the Island of Hayti, with climate
reasonably suited to white labor, can furnish cotton for the present consumption of the world. A few years' continuance of the
war, by the high prices resulting from the sudden loss of the
American crop, will stimulate the production of the staple in numerous parts of the world where it is not now raised, and then
the southern monopoly will be gone, and with it will go southern
slavery forever. Without cotton, what is slavery worth?

Never have I known such an infatuation as that of the slaveholders destroying the Union to save slavery. It was never so
safe as under the ægis of the Constitution of the United States.
In this Union, it has "flourished like the green bay tree," and it
has flourished nowhere else. I think the views I earnestly pressed
upon our legislature just before the State seceded, and often before, are those which should have governed the slaveholders of
the south. I said:

"In my judgment, there is no safety for this institution save in the Constitution of
the United States. There it is recognised and protected. No other property is speci-
ally protected. Slaves are represented; no other property is. This Union of ours is
the great bulwark of slavery. Nowhere else has it flourished; and, break up the
6

Union when you will, you knock away its strongest prop. A Southern Confederacy will be to it its deadliest blast, if not its grave. The whole civilized world is intensely hostile to slavery; and the moment a new confederacy is formed, based on the single idea of slavery, numerous and malignant antagonisms will be evoked which may endanger the institution. But, under the shield of the Constitution of the United States, these antagonisms, whether foreign or domestic, are, and ever will be, harmless. In that blessed instrument it is a recognised institution—part and parcel of our frame of government, and of our social and industrial systems—to the protection of which the entire power of the great Government of the United States stands pledged before the entire world. Thus secure under the wing of the Union, why shall we risk its security by rushing on untried experiments?"

Yes, why should we? Why expose it to the exacting and perilous necessities of war? Why let it go within reach of a whirlpool, whose strong vortex may sweep down its bark, and submerge it forever?

Another exception I am constrained to take to pursuing the course my State prescribes me, is, that she has transferred me to, and made me a citizen of, the Confederate States, without giving me a chance of indicating my assent or dissent. Bound hand and foot, I am sold to South Carolina, for *she* did the "dragging." I dispute the fairness of the sale; I impeach the indentures for fraud; and if I *am* to be sold, I want the poor privilege of choosing my master. I shudder at the thought of being sold to South Carolina. For near forty years she has been a disturber of the national peace; for near forty years she has never caught one inspiration from the stars and stripes. She is a wicked, seditious State. *She* hates the Union; *I* love it with all my soul. Let me never—oh! let me never be turned over to such a State! Let me be a Russian surf, rather! And then, to think of Virginia—once proud Virginia—the "mother of States and statesmen"—the land of stirring memories and "bright particular" renown—crouched at the footstool of South Carolina!!!

One more reason why I could not venture the fatal leap of secession. I had not the courage—I frankly own I wanted the courage. When Walpole, a prime minister of Great Britain, was taunted with an unwillingness to tax America, he replied: "I will leave that measure to some one of my successors who has more courage than I have." And so say I. I leave this dangerous, awful thing of secession to those who have more courage than I

claim to possess. And I trust that those who have shown more
courage in this matter than I could summon, will not have occasion to be reminded of the ill-fated history of the Grenville min-
istry, that, having more courage than Pitt and Walpole, did
undertake to tax America, and, by so doing, lost to England the
brightest jewel in her Crown.

When I thought on the unhappy consequences that, I plainly
foresaw, would come upon my State and her people; when I saw,
as plainly as I ever saw God's sun in the heavens, that if Virginia seceded, her territory would become the theatre of a devas-
tating war, and she and her citizens the chief sufferers by it,
while the guiltier parties who had brought it on would repose in
the shade of comparative peace and ease; when I reflected that
an absolute ruin of all her vital interests was inevitable; that her
grand system of internal improvements—her future hope—would
lie a heap of prostrate ruins; that repudiation even would be her
doom by the exhausting effects of an exhausting war; that her
people would, by blockade, be cut off from the markets of the
world, their comforts abridged, the price of all the necessaries of
life advanced to insufferable rates, and the burdens of taxation
crushing down the energies of her tax-payers; that all the poor
people of her tide-water region, whose subsistence was derived
almost exclusively from the northern trade, would be reduced to
starvation; that she would lose, in the first month of secession,
two hundred millions of dollars in her slave property alone;
when I contemplated the penury, and want, and suffering of the
humble poor which war brings with infallible certainty for that
more helpless class; the social desolation, the broken hearts, the
helpless widowhood and orphanage, the severance of all the dear,
sweet ties of life, the burning hates, the alienation of bosom from
bosom, the "death-feud's enmities" which can die only at the
point of the piercing sword, the separation of husbands and wives,
and fathers and mothers, and sons and daughters, the blood and
death of war's sad havoc: I say, when I thought of all these
inevitable consequences of secession, my courage sank, and I
resolved—I know now I was right—to have my skirts clear and
my hands clean when the day of retribution should come.

Caius Marius, at the end of one of the civil wars that had wasted

44

the blood and substance of Rome, was forced to sink himself up
to the chin in the marshes of Minturna, to escape recognition and
the vengeance of his wronged and ruined countrymen. I have
no ambition, nor do I mean, to have the fate of Marius mine.

Another consideration, of itself controlling, moves me against
secession. In God's name, what does the south want with independence? It is no boon—it will prove a fearful and enduring curse.

Provision for self-destruction being expressly made in the constitution of the Confederate States, by conceding to each of the
confederating parties the right to withdraw at will, what can the
Government end in but convulsing changes and revolutions, de-
structive of all material advancement, and of all social quiet and
happiness? Can such a Government last a lustrum? Can it, for
example, confine within its restraints even for five short years, the
turbulent spirit of South Carolina? Such a Government is no Government. It is not worth a rush.

And if all history be not at fault, border wars will be inevitable,
and a taxation, to protect a long frontier, which would destroy
the substance, and paralyze the energies, of any people on earth.

The next bitter fruit will be entangling alliances with foreign
powers, perhaps abject dependence on them, or, may be, ultimate
subjugation.

But this branch of the subject I turn over to a master limner,
the Hon. Jere. Clemens, of Alabama, who spoke thus to the people of Huntsville, during the last presidential canvass:

"If secession could be peaceably effected—if the northern and southern States
could be by common consent divided into two separate confederacies—if not one
drop of blood was spilled, or one blade of grass destroyed, in making the change,
it would still bring unnumbered evils in its train. There would be a standing army
to be maintained of not less than 50,000 men, at a cost of $50,000,000 per annum.
A navy must be built up, and the money for that purpose dragged from the pockets of
the people. There would be a long line of frontier extending from the Atlantic ocean
to the western limits of Missouri, and from the northern boundary of that State to the
Rio Grande, which it would be necessary to stud with military posts, and every mile
of which would require to be secured by armed patrols, for the double purpose of
enforcing the revenue laws, and preventing the escape of fugitive slaves. Every har-
bor along the vast extent of sea coast, from Delaware Bay to the Rio Grande, would
require an appropriation of millions for its fortifications. The people would be
ground down by taxes, and demoralized by the constant presence of troops in their
midst, who acknowledged no restraints but those of military law. Incessant quarrels
would grow up between you and your northern neighbors, and bloody wars would

desolate your frontiers, if they did not spread destruction throughout every portion of your territory.

The dream of a Southern Confederacy is the wildest vision that ever troubled the brain of a moon-struck enthusiast; a dream interrupted by bloody conflicts with your neighbors, and a vile dependence on a foreign power."

As for the other condition on which I may be safe in Virginia, the taking of the oath of allegiance to the Confederate States of America, I spurn it with infinite scorn. I would sooner rot in a dungeon than swear any such fealty.

This Government of the Confederate States of America I regard as the grandest, most stupendous, foulest fraud known in the history of the world. It is no government of the people. The people had no part nor lot in the matter. It was, as to the cotton States at least, the precipitation of discontented or ambitious spirits, that sought no redress for actual grievances, but who, for a higher civilization, or a pure slave republic, or some other Utopian project, longed to break down the government. "All changes in the fundamental law of a State, (said Mr. Calhoun) ought to be the work of time, ample discussion, and reflection." But how was it with the formation of this Southern Confederacy? The South Carolina convention met on the 17th of December, 1860, and on the 20th, she was out of the Union. And, in less than four months, eight stars had been struck from the national standard. A government which it had cost our fathers seven years of hard fighting, and as many of hard experience and sober reflection to create, in four short months dashed into ruins! And this without the people being allowed the poor privilege of saying whether they would or would not sanction the vandalism! I can swear by no such government. Nor do I desire to live, or have my children live, under a government which contains, in the very first paragraph of its constitution, the principle of dissolution. Give me, rather, a government under which I and mine will have some guarantee for safety to property and for stability in all the rights of society, some safeguard against fickle change and destroying revolution. Give me the old Union—the Union of Washington and Madison, and Franklin, and not this poor abortion of Davis, Yancey, and Rhett, which,

"Like the Borealis race,
That flits ere you can find the place,"

may be here to-day, and forever gone to-morrow!

In truth, this struggle on the part of the loyal States, is a struggle for the very existence of the institution of property, and of all government itself. As such, it ought to be, and must be, met.

For one, I cannot listen to the dulcet strain which comes up from the south on a thousand strings, that this struggle of the cotton States is a struggle for the great principles of civil liberty. To put it on so honorable a basis, is bold imposture. The Constitution of the United States is the best system of civil liberty that ever emanated from human hearts and heads. It is the accumulated political wisdom of the world, from the time of Magna Charta to 1789. Those who would subvert it, are no friends to civil liberty. They are strangers to the spirit of Hampden, and Russell, and Pym, and Algernon Sidney, and Washington, and Hancock, and Otis, and Thatcher, and Madison, and Clay, and Webster. Yet more unblushing is the effrontery which would liken the contest in which the Confederate States are engaged, to the struggle for Colonial liberty in the Revolution. The comparison is almost profanity. It utterly falsifies history. The great principle of the American Revolution was, that taxation and representation should not be dis-united. The Colonies contended that unless they were represented, they should not be taxed— that they who paid the taxes, should have a voice in their imposition. Is any such principle involved in the present conflict? Was ever the right claimed to tax the southern people without representation? Has the Federal Government ever made the effort to deprive them of representation? *Before* secession, had not the now seceded States full representation in the Congress—a representation of all white citizens, and three-fifths of all others, including slaves? And, by virtue of that representation, has not the south nearly all the time controlled and shaped the Federal legislation and policy? Did not South Carolina herself, through her Calhoun and Lowndes, and other representatives, even fix upon New England the protective system? And how does the south now lose her representation in the National Legislature, but by her own silly, suicidal act of secession? And how has she fallen into her present position of peril, war, desolation, and ruin, but by seceding and giving up her representation in Congress? Whose fault is it that she is unrepresented?

And how is it, except by the abdication of her rightful representation, that she is now placed within reach of confiscation and emancipation?

Such are the reasons that forbid me to be a secessionist.

And I think my old friends in Virginia ought to pardon me for my great love of the Union, for I have had some good teachers among her distinguished sons, whose precepts I have never forgotten, and never shall forget. I quote, as the last section of this long defence, the following patriotic, immortal sentiments:

" When your fathers attempted to form this Union, they did not know, beforehand, what sort of a Union it was to be.

" They set to work, and did the best they could under the circumstances.

" What they would accomplish no man could tell. There was not a head upon either of them that had the human wisdom to foretell what it was to be ; but they went in for Union for Union's sake.

" By all the Gods, by all the altars of my country, I go for Union for Union's sake. They set to work to make the best Union they could, and they did make the best Union and the best Government that ever was made.

" Washington, Franklin, Jefferson,—all combined, in Congress or out of Congress, in Convention or out of Convention, never made that Constitution—God Almighty sent it down to your fathers. It was a work, too, of glory, and a work of inspiration.

" I believe that as fully as I believe in my Bible. No man, from Hamilton, and Jay, and Madison—from Edmund Randolph, who had the chief hand in making it—and he was a Virginian—the writers of it, the authors of it, and you have lived under it from 1789 to this year of our Lord 1858, and none of your fathers, and none of your fathers' sons have ever measured the height, or the depth, or the length, or the breadth, of the wisdom of that Constitution."

These are the words—of whom? Of one of Virginia's favorite and most gifted sons—Henry A. Wise. They should be read every day in every American school, and be gotten by heart by every American youth. Long, long may they animate the American heart!

And now, I shall take the liberty, in return for the uncharitable judgment and abundant denunciation which have been my lot in my native land, to venture to my fellow-citizens there a little advice, which, however unthankfully received, is honestly tendered.

Give up this ill-omened and ruinous war. Require your lawgivers at once to adopt the amendment proposed by Congress to the Constitution to prohibit all interference with slavery in the States, and then return to your loyalty and to the Union of old.

And I assign two brief reasons for the admonition. First, if this war be not speedily terminated, the institution of southern slavery perishes forever—not by the willing acts of the Federal Government, but by the current of irresistible events—a consequence, not an object of the war, for which secession alone will be responsible. The highest interest of the slaveholders, if they desire to preserve their peculiar institution, is, THE SPEEDIEST POSSIBLE TERMINATION OF THE WAR. Secondly, persistance in this struggle is vain. There is one reason establishing its vanity, independent of all others, and that is, that the people of the Mississippi valley must have the free navigation of the " great father of waters," and will have it at every hazard, and will fight for it, while a drop of western blood remains. They *will* have it, I repeat. It is a geographical necessity, totally irresistible. The States of the lower Mississippi and those above, *must* belong to a common government. There can be no divided empire there. Unless the people of Virginia, then, are prepared to carry on this unnatural and wasting contest until the last western man—a race as brave as their southern brethren, and capable of far more physical endurance—has fallen in his tracks, they had better at once throw down the arms of rebellion, and return to the Government under which they were always prosperous and happy, and under which their State was so rapidly advancing to power and grandeur.

This long letter I have written as a defence of my course. I desire to let my fellow-citizens of Virginia see that, while I have not been able to go with my State at this trying crisis, I have, at least, respectable reasons " for the faith that is in me." I trust you will make an effort to get it into some of the papers of the State, that this my defence may be known. It will be at least a consolation to my family, and to the few cherished friends, whom neither the troubles of the times nor defamation have estranged.

Affectionately,

JOS. SEGAR.

www.ingramcontent.com/pod-product-compliance
Lightning Source LLC
Chambersburg PA
CBHW030723110426
42739CB00030B/1359